T0197142

"STAY FOCUSED ON THE LIGHT"

Written by: Zoe A Gable
Inspired by the Holy Spirit: On 06/13/04

ZOE A GABLE

authorHOUSE®

AuthorHouse™
1663 Liberty Drive
Bloomington, IN 47403
www.authorhouse.com
Phone: 833-262-8899

Published by AuthorHouse 11/08/2022

ISBN: 978-1-6655-7524-9 (sc)
ISBN: 978-1-6655-7522-5 (hc)
ISBN: 978-1-6655-7523-2 (e)

Library of Congress Control Number: 2022920806

Print information available on the last page.

CONTENTS

PREFACE

Have you ever had such an awful day where nothing seems to go right? You feel like the whole world is crashing in all around you and you just want to throw in the towel and say to heck with it? Then all of a sudden just when you start to give up, something wonderful happens that makes you forget about your awful day? That is what happened to me on 06/13/2004 around 11:00 p.m.

I remember it like it was yesterday! I remember fighting with my husband, fighting with my co-workers, mad at my puppy for chewing up things like my music cd's, and many other things that had upset me that day. I was so stressed out and depressed. All I wanted to do was cry. I kept trying to move forward and clean house but my heart was not in anything. I remember lying down and starting to cry and then all of a sudden, I heard the Lord's voice! He said:

"STAY FOCUSED ON THE LIGHT!!"

Instantly my emotional pain was gone. I felt full of His joy and love. I was smiling. I was so overcome by His words that I had completely forgotten about the bad events that had happened that day completely! His words became my primary focus! I went to bed that night smiling and full of His peace in my heart.

As the days passed, I began to understand His words. I began to realize that I was causing my own unhappiness. I was thinking on negative things and focusing on the wrong things. His few words inspired me! It did not take much but those few words showed me how to be happy. All I had to do was change my thoughts and focus. If I wanted to be happy, I had to focus and think on happier things.

In middle school, before I became a Christian, I had always dreamed of being a writer. I had written short stories, plays, poems, and even some songs. I fantasized about writing musicals and having them portrayed on Broadway. I even dreamed of starring in them!

As it drew closer to my high school graduation day, I started pursuing schools where I could pursue my dream. Unfortunately too many people discouraged me. They would tell me that writing was a hobby, not a job or career. I had to find something else. I was devastated. I could not think of anything else I wanted to do! I applied at several colleges but was unsure of what to put down for majors. I ended up picking majors in employment fields that I thought those people would approve of. When I went to college and took those courses, I did alright in many of them but failed at others. I honestly did not care about my grades that much. I was secretly sad because my heart was not in what I was doing. I just basically went through the motions. I went to class and did my homework. I did not enjoy anything and I felt like a robot.

After college, I went through the same routine. I applied at jobs I thought they would approve of but all the while hating the work. I was always miserable. I went through so many jobs and never enjoyed any of them. For me having a job was just a way of paying the bills. I was not supposed to enjoy it or be happy. I did not care what I did as long as the bills got paid. I would just tell myself that someday when I had free time or was able to retire, I would write again but as you can imagine that time never came . . .until now.

In August of 2014 my health went downhill. I found myself in a wheelchair and unable to leave the couch much. The Lord started speaking to me again and He reminded me of His words in 2004. I felt like it was finally time to start writing. Due to my health problems, I was in the perfect position to write because I could not do anything else!

As the months went by however different things kept interfering with my writing. My health was always so poor that I slept most days and I also began suffering from great pain. In late 2014, my health got so bad that my only form of mobilization was a wheelchair. Family members had to drive me to appointments and spend every day with me to make sure I was taken care of. My doctors kept sending me to different specialists and I learned that my immune system was compromised. In total I had seven or eight different doctors that I saw regularly. I eventually had to give up working all together and file for disability. As you can imagine I became severely depressed and wondered if I would ever be able to do anything again. Since that time the Lord has been working on healing me. I am out of the wheelchair now and as you can see, I have started writing again.

The ideas for this book came from His words back in 2004 and from His constant inspiration. I have always dreamed of writing a book ever since I was little but never could decide on a topic or genre to write about. He helped me discover the topic and gave me the encouragement I needed to complete this task. He was always there to remind me time and time again of how my thoughts affect my happiness. He often used sermons, songs, and motivation from others to encourage me to write this book. I would feel His tug the strongest when I would hear sermons on sharing testimony. He was basically telling me to share my story with you. I guess you could say this is my testimony but I feel more inclined to say; however, that I want to help others with my experiences.

The Lord has taught me so many things over the last few years. I have never been good at preaching or ministry. I could never say the right words out loud to others. Every time I tried, fear would get in the way. My best mode of communication has always been the written word. It is hard to explain but I can express myself better in writing and I feel freer to open up more. I never would have dreamed that I would write a book on my story though. I always pictured myself writing fantasy or romance novels but I guess He had other plans!

Throughout this book, I will share my experiences with you. I will warn you; however that many of these experiences may be hard to read. I only say this now so as not to shock you later on. I will also share Bible verses and poems that I have written. I include all of these because they have always helped me and I pray they will help you as well.

We never know what the future holds for us. God has so many things in store for us and many of those things do not necessarily line up with our own plans. I hope someday though if by chance you do find yourself in a similar predicament, please let my words guide or encourage you. If you do not take my words to heart then I pray more so that you take His words into consideration. He was there for me during my darkest of days as well as my happiest of moments. He has never left my side, even when I left His. I may not always have followed Him as closely as I should have but He always believed in me and stayed by my side. He believed in me even when I did not believe in myself. I pray and know that He will also always be there for you!

God bless you on your journey. I pray that He will give you all that your heart desires. I also pray that you remain strong. Keep the faith and do not let your heart stray from Him. If He speaks to you, please listen, obey His voice and stay focused on the Light. Thank you.

INTRODUCTION

After much deliberation and prayer, I decided to divide my book into three sections or parts. I include many different topics in my book and I felt that the different sections would better divide the topics for better understanding. I felt this method was better as well because each section deals with different stages in my life. The first section deals with pain and heartache. The second part deals with finding joy and happiness and lastly, the third part will encourage and uplift. I also discuss lessons I have learned in these sections. I felt the division would help the reader better understand my journey as well as learn and grow.

To further elaborate on Part 1 of my book, I discuss numerous events that occurred in my childhood. As all childhoods begin, I decided to list events as they occurred in time beginning with my early years. I wanted to express how my emotional state was affected by each challenge I faced and how that affected the next stage in my life.

As I grew older, once again I was confronted with trials. I explain how those trials affected me emotionally and how I tried to deal with the situation. Many people deal with different situations every day but we do not normally speak out loud the thought processes we have in our head during those times. I want to be completely open and honest with my readers. I want them to really understand the pain and confusion I went through. I can almost guarantee that many of my readers will have had similar thoughts at different points in their life.

As I move on to Chapters 4 and 5 in this section, I begin to include experiences in high school and later college. Once again I dealt with many decisions and heartache. I met many different types of people during this point and I learned how heartbreaking people can be. My emotional state really began to unravel during this point and I share the many different ways I coped with these situations. I finally found a glimpse of hope in high school and college but it was short lived. At the time, I was not strong enough to cope with it. I began to really fall apart and I felt constantly lost and confused.

Not all of the sections in my book are negative, however. In Part 2, I discuss how I found hope and happiness. I began to be more positive and I share how I started to see things a little differently. I also explain how I found the Lord and how He really began to turn my life around. Being a Christian does not mean that I will never again find heartache or face emotional pain but it does give me a better way to handle it. It changes my outlook on every situation and gives me strength during trials.

I was faced with more challenges during this time but I share how His love and Word helped me learn and grow from these trials. I found strength in myself that I never knew I had. I had begun to see myself in an entirely new light. The lessons He taught me during this time period also helped me to evolve into a better person. I began to make friends and I learned how to build relationships. I learned daily from His teaching and by doing so, I became a stronger and happier person.

In Part 3, I share with you a few things that the Lord actually taught me while I was writing this book. He has taught me many lessons throughout my life but I learned the most from Him while writing this book.

One topic He pressed the most on my heart was to write about thoughts and focus. This section discusses the power of our thoughts and focus. As I was doing the research for these topics, He revealed to me new insight daily. I learned how thoughts and focus really determined how happy I was. I was amazed at how many times my thoughts and focus remained on the wrong things. As I began to examine myself more closely, I learned how I really was sabotaging my own happiness and I strived continuously afterwards to become a better person. I began analyzing my thoughts more closely and often forced myself to focus on happier things.

The final chapters of my book in this section really express the importance of a walk with Christ. I wanted my words to lead others down a much happier, more fulfilling road. I hope that my words will encourage others to reach out and change their own happiness. All they need to do is change their heart. Taking risks and being vulnerable is often hard to do but the rewards are worth it. I have never regretted my choice. If I did have any regrets, it would be that I did not find Him sooner. Why was I so rebellious? Why was I so stubborn? I may have avoided many of the same mistakes and shed less tears if I had not resisted Him so often.

I only want my book to be an inspiration to others. It does not matter to me how much I make off of writing or how many people actually read the book. The only thing that I care about is touching at least one person. I know that there must be at least one person out there that may have had similar circumstances. Maybe that person is still suffering. Maybe they do not know how to heal. I only hope that my lessons and words of encouragement will find that one person and touch their heart. I would love to lead that person down the right road to follow. If I can accomplish this one thing, I will feel like everything that I have endured was worth it in the end.

I dedicate this book to my husband. He has always supported me and encouraged me during the whole writing process. Even when I got busy and put off writing, he always pushed me to keep going and I would not have been able to complete my dream without his love and support.

PART 1

PAST PAIN THAT LED TO MY DOWNFALL

CHAPTER 1

The Beginning Of Sorrows

Has anyone ever given you a penny and asked you for your thoughts? No one has ever done that to me but if anyone ever did, I would have to say that my thoughts used to dwell too much on my past and on very negative things. I admit that I still struggle with this some days but with the Lord's help, I am improving. It is one part of me that I wish I could erase completely.

"A penny for your thoughts:" that phrase always stuck with me. I am not sure why but I always wondered where it originated. I did some research on the topic. Many people do not say it much anymore but I heard it a lot when I was younger. A "penny for your thoughts" is an English phrase. It was used to encourage people to share their opinions on issues being discussed. I am unclear if money actually changed hands during this time but regardless, a penny is not much to pay to share your thoughts.

The credit for the phrase goes to a man by the name of John Heywood. He was born just before the 16th century. He wrote many plays and a book in 1546, known as *A dialogue conteinying the nomber in effect of all the proverbes in the Englishe tongue[1]*. Mr. Heywood did not develop the phrase personally but he was the earliest person found so far to have used the phrase in writing. Although the original origin of the phrase is unknown, it does date back to around the end of the Middle Ages.

Back in that day, the worth of a penny was a lot more than it is today. The phrase made people feel appreciated because it was like saying their opinions mattered and they were worth a lot to the person hearing them. Today however, because the value of the penny has dropped dramatically, the phrase would be construed as an insult rather than a compliment. It was especially insulting if the phrase was given in a sarcastic tone.

As I mentioned earlier, if you offered a penny for my thoughts, you would learn about my past. In my heart I feel as though my past has been one continual disappointment or heartache after another. Please do not misunderstand me. I do not include my upbringing in this generalization but mostly events that have occurred outside of the family and my upbringing. I personally feel that my upbringing was wonderful and I am very blessed in that regard, especially if compared to others close to me. In terms of events that have transpired outside of my family; however, it is a completely different story.

---

[1] Black, Ken. "What Does 'a Penny for Your Thoughts' Mean?" Conjecture Corporation, wiseGEEK. Revised By: G. Wiesen and Edited By: Bronwyn Harris, 09 March 2015, www.wisegeek.org/what-does-a-penny-for-your-thoughts-mean.htm.

I am in my 40's now and as I look back over my past, I have a different view of it than what may have been the case about ten years ago. The Lord has really helped me to see things in a new light. As you can see, it took years for me to really examine myself, my past, and my accomplishments and try to determine from that what would be considered as blessings. True I may never actually receive physical blessings from my past experiences but the lessons my past has taught me and the personality I have developed over the years have really shown me that maybe pain, as hard as it might be, is a blessing in and of itself.

It all began when I was around 6 or 7 years old. My family and I were living in large city in a singlewide trailer located in a very populated trailer park. I do not have a very large family. It consists of just my parents, my younger brother and sister, and me. At this particular point in time however my brother was not yet born.

One day my parents went off to work and left my sister and me with a babysitter. There were other kids there and she and I had fun playing with them outside in the yard. I remember an older girl there who every child adored. They struggled hard to try to impress her and did everything in their power to be her friend. For the protection of identities and the sake of the story, I will call her Amy.

I do not remember much about Amy other than she had blonde hair and she seemed to have a speaking disability of some sort. She also had a very close friend by the name of Becky that was always there at the babysitters' house as well. They were practically inseparable. I never really had any problems with Amy or Becky. They always seemed to treat me nice and I thought they both liked me. Unfortunately, it was not until much later that I learned that Becky hated me and to this day I am not real sure why or what I had done to her.

I remember playing in the sand box with some other kids when Becky and Amy came over to talk to me. They acted so nice to me and I was excited because I felt I had made new friends. Shortly thereafter my mom arrived to pick us up from the babysitters. I was having fun though and did not want to leave. My mom came over by where I was and told me that it was time to go. Amy asked my mom if it would be okay if I came over one night to have a sleepover at her house. I got excited and begged my mom to let me go. At first my mom said that I was too young for a sleepover but when I told her that I really wanted to go and after much persuasion and begging, she finally agreed.

Honestly I do not remember exactly how long after that day did the actual sleepover take place but I believe it was that same weekend or the weekend after. I remember mom dropping me off at Amy's house and being so excited. It was my very first sleepover and I was invited by the most popular girl at the babysitter's house. All I could think about was how everyone would talk when they found out I was here! I would have so many friends and I would be so popular too!

The evening at her house went wonderful! We watched movies, ate pizza, had root beer floats, and played games. She had a younger brother as well and afterwards, we went upstairs and played hide and seek. We also played dress up in her mother's clothes. It was so much fun.

As it started to grow late, her father yelled upstairs that we needed to settle down and get ready for bed. We began to take off her mother's dresses and put the toys away. While we were preparing for bed, Amy came up to me and asked me if I wanted to play another game with her. I told her that we were supposed to go to bed now. She said that it was a quiet game in the bed. I got excited and said sure! I asked her what it was called and she said that it was a master/servant game and she was the master and I was the servant. Basically I was supposed to do whatever she told me do. I told her the game sounded like fun as long as I got to be the master once too. She agreed and we got ready to play.

As we were heading into the bed, Amy's brother came into the room. He asked me what we were going to do now and I told him about the master/servant game. He looked at me very strange and said the words I will never forget: "When my sister plays that game with other kids, she makes them do weird and sick things."

After he said that, I began to get scared and worried. I wasn't sure what to expect but I knew I didn't like what he told me. I was afraid of what she would tell me to do. Amy then yelled at her brother to "shut up and go away." After he left the room, Amy and I climbed into bed.

"Are you ready to play?" Amy asked.

"I . . . ugh . . . guess so." I replied hesitantly. I seriously contemplated saying no to her at this point but I thought I should give her the benefit of the doubt. What if her brother was only messing with me? What if he was just trying to scare me?

"Good. First, I order you to lick my pussy and suck on my boobs." She demanded.

"What?!" I asked shockingly.

"You heard me! Do as I command!" She ordered.

I instantly jumped out of the bed and told her no! I told her that I would not do that because it was wrong.

"If you don't do it, I will tell my parents on you and they will call your mom and tell her that you were misbehaving and you will never be allowed to come over again!" She threatened.

Now that I look back on it, if I had it to do over again, I would have told her at that moment to go ahead and call my mom because I would rather go home. Instead, I was naïve and scared. I seriously thought I would get into a lot of trouble. I also wasn't entirely sure who was in the wrong. It felt wrong to me but I wasn't really taught much about sex at this point and didn't understand if what I was feeling was right or wrong. I didn't know it at the time but what Amy was asking me to do was <u>very seriously wrong</u>. I mean, I <u>was</u> only 6 or 7 years old! I felt it was wrong inside but I was unsure of myself. All I knew was that I was just a kid and she was older than me. Maybe she knew more than I did and I didn't want to get into trouble.

I slowly climbed back into the bed with her and went between her legs. She used her hand and pushed my face into her crotch. I didn't know what I was doing at the time. I just stuck out my tongue and moved it around. It felt so sick and wrong and I hated being there. Not to mention, it was very gross.

After that, she forced me up to her boobs and I did the same thing with my tongue. After several minutes, which felt to me like hours, she said that I did "good" and we could go to sleep now. She rolled over and went to sleep. I just laid there staring at the ceiling.

I remember that I did not sleep much that night. My mind kept racing and I felt so scared and uneasy for what had just happened. I wasn't sure what scared me more: what I had done to her or what would have happened if it never would have happened at all. The next morning was a blur. I was quiet. I didn't talk to anyone and Amy acted just like she won a battle. She was extra excited and pretended like nothing ever happened. I didn't understand her behavior. Her brother came up to me and asked if Amy had forced me to play the game. I told him yes.

"I told you so." He replied.

I should've listened to him. If anything, I should've asked him for more specifics about what the game was. Maybe if I would've known what to expect, I would've been more prepared. I would've known what to say to her when she told me what to do. I could've called my mom and asked her to come and get me and take me home.

It was almost time to go home. I was waiting for my mom to pull up when Amy came up beside me:

"If you EVER tell anyone what happened last night, I will KILL you!" She demanded.

"Oh . . . ok . . . I won't." I stammered. Her tone scared me. I didn't know what to do or what to say. I was terrified.

"I am serious!" She yelled as she walked away.

I turned back to the window to watch for my mother with tears in my eyes. Her actions and tone really scared me. She was bigger and older than me too. I didn't know what to do. I honestly believed that she WOULD kill me!

My mother came and picked me up later that day and I was too scared to tell her what had happened. I climbed in the car and put my seat belt on. She then turned and asked if I had fun. I simply said yes and stared out of the window. I never said a word the whole ride home. I didn't know what to tell her. I was afraid of getting in trouble. I thought that if she knew what had happened, she would get mad at me – like it was my entire fault. I wouldn't blame her for getting mad at me. I blamed myself for what happened. I was very young after all and I wasn't real sure what was right and what was wrong. I was also scared of Amy. If she found out that I told my mom, she would kill me! I knew that what Amy forced me to do felt wrong somehow but I was never told what to do in that situation. I felt guilty and dirty. I felt like a bad person. I was afraid that my mom would think that way about me too.

As if that wasn't bad enough, Amy had to add insult to injury. Unbeknownst to me, Amy had told Becky what had happened between her and me. The only difference is that she exaggerated the story quite a bit. She told Becky that I raped her and forced myself on her. Amy said she screamed and I hit her and refused to let her go. Becky decided to take it upon herself to inform the entire school of Amy's exaggerated version.

I remember walking onto the school grounds that following Monday morning and every kid there just stopping and staring at me weirdly. I didn't know what was going on. I just felt every eye staring at me. I slowly walked over to my best friend Beth and asked her what was going on. She said that she couldn't be friends with me anymore and that I was a sick pervert. She immediately walked into the school with Becky. I kept asking Beth after that what was going on. I still didn't understand why she acted that way and why everyone was staring at me. Later that day, she met me alone in the classroom while everyone was out on recess and explained to me what Becky had told everyone. I began to cry. I told her that it was all a lie and that I didn't do any of that.

"Is all of it really a lie?" She asked.

"Yes! It didn't happen like that at all! I did stay at Amy's house and we did do things to some degree but not the way Becky told it. Amy forced <u>me</u> to do those things to her. I didn't force Amy. I tried to tell her no but she threatened me." I replied crying. "I don't know why Becky is telling it the other way around."

"Quit lying! You are a sick pervert and I don't want to be friends with you anymore!" Beth yelled.

"I am not lying, Beth! I swear! It's Becky that's lying!" I cried to her.

"Even if that were true, we still can't be friends anymore. I can't trust you anymore." She said quietly. After that, she left the classroom and went outside, leaving me all alone. I sat down at my desk and cried.

I tried so hard after that to make pictures and cards for Beth. I tried everything I could think of to impress her and apologize to her. I wanted to make her see that I was telling the truth but no matter what I did, she ignored me or threw the things I made away. She ended up being best friends with Becky. Everyone in the school hated me and I was always alone at recess. No one would ever talk to me and I always sat alone on the swings at recess time crying. Many kids would laugh at me and play mean pranks on me. I felt hated everywhere I went.

Shortly before the school year was over for the summer, my parents informed me that we would be moving to a small town. They had purchased a bowling alley there and we would be starting a new school in the fall. At first I was sad to leave my "used-to-be" friends behind, but deep down inside I was thankful. I was thankful for the chance to start over and meet new people. I was hoping that the kids at the new school didn't hear about what had happened here.

As the school year drew towards a close, I grew more and more excited. I wanted to move so badly! I couldn't wait! I think my parents were shocked to find that I wasn't more upset about moving. I couldn't tell them why I was excited though. They didn't even know what really happened between Amy and me! How could I tell them about the rumor going around school? All I knew was that I just wanted to put everything behind me and start over at a new school. The sooner we got out of there, the happier I was!

CHAPTER 2

Childhood Hurts

We moved to a very small town about a thirty-forty minute drive from where we used to live. There was only one main street with few businesses and a courthouse. They didn't even have a McDonald's! My parents rented this awesome little 2-story house right in town behind a grocery store. My next door neighbor was the same age as I was and his name was Joe. I may have been only about 9 or 10 years old at the time, but I still thought he was cute!

My parents had made an arrangement with Joe's parents. Joe and his little brother walked my sister and I to school every morning. My mom didn't feel comfortable with my sister and I walking to school alone. It was about 2-3 blocks from our house to the school and my mom didn't want us walking by ourselves.

Joe was my age and in my grade and his brother was my sister's age and in her grade. Every morning the four of us walked to school together. I remember arriving at school one morning and several girls in my class came up to me. They acted so jealous because I got to walk with Joe every day. He was the most popular kid in our school and all of the girls adored him.

True at first I thought he was cute but after I got to know him, I began to learn what kind of a jerk he was. He treated girls poorly and cut them down all of the time. He would call me names and play pranks on me. If I was taking out the trash, he would throw things over the fence at me. I began to hate him so much and when girls would come up to me and act jealous, I would tell them that he was a jerk and they could have him.

As the years went by my mom no longer required that Joe and his brother walk us to school and my sister and I began to walk by ourselves. As you can imagine the first time walking alone without Joe was pretty scary. Even though I did not like Joe anymore, I felt safer walking with him and found myself starting to actually miss him. I was thankful though that one of the girls that would come up to me asking about Joe lived in a large house on the same path we walked to school and I began to meet up with her every morning. I began walking with her and her younger brother to school every morning.

I have to admit that this new school was definitely better than where I used to be. My favorite subjects were Math and English and I was able to make a lot of great friends. I never complained about my grades either. True I was never an all A student but I always worked hard and even though my GPA was only roughly 3.2, I felt proud and happy. I was actually accomplishing something. I was just happy to have friends again and forget about the chaos at the other school.

It wasn't until I reached the age of 12 that things began to change again. All of a sudden, I started my period for the first time. I also had to start wearing bras. What made matters worse, was that I was already in a "B" cup. I was larger than all of the girls in my class. In fact, many of the girls in my class didn't even have boobs! My mom kept reassuring me though that it was normal and they would grow boobs too eventually. I was just an early bloomer and it runs in the family. As annoyed as I was, I understood.

About a house or two down from us, there lived an African American male. He was a couple of years younger than I was but very tall for his age. In fact he was taller than I was and looked older than I did. I started getting scared to walk to school because he would wait for me to leave my house and knock me down. I would try to get away from him but he would pin me down and give me tity twisters. I started having a hard time leaving my house every morning and my mom would have to yell at me and force me to go. I tried to tell her what was going on but she said that I was just making stuff up and I needed to get going.

One day I was standing by the front door looking out the front window for him. When I thought the coast was clear, I tried to make a break for it and began to run to school. Unfortunately, he was hiding behind a tree and he began to chase after me. He eventually caught up to me and tackled me to the ground again. He was on top of me giving me titty twisters when my mother finally saw what had happened and yelled at him. He immediately got off me and ran away. Thankfully, that was the last time I ever saw him.

Even though that topic was pretty much closed as far as my mom was concerned, I could still feel the insecurities and emotional stress the events played in my mind. I began to hate my body and I started not trusting anyone — especially boys. I started always wearing turtle necks, sweaters, etc. that made sure to conceal my body as best I could. I tried hard to focus on schoolwork and ignore anything else but found myself getting overwhelmed by constant attention by boys in my school. I was the only girl in the class that had boobs. I could not wait for the day when other girls would get them too so the boys would leave me alone.

CHAPTER 3

The Next Big Pain

I wish some days that I could say that boys and my body was the only thing left to deal with growing up and that the rest of my life was happy but unfortunately I would be premature in doing so. What can someone say about their childhood? For many people they play, go to school, do their homework, do their chores, etc. They do the same old boring things every day. Yes in the summer they may go camping, swimming, etc. but when the fall comes it's the same old routine again. It may sound boring or simple but I do have to say that sometimes I wish I was still a kid. I didn't have to have a job or pay bills. I didn't have many responsibilities. Those were the days!

As much as I wish I could still be a kid though, I am very thankful that I am not because I didn't think my childhood was all that great. Yes my home life with my parents and siblings was wonderful but again outside of the home life made me thankful that my childhood was over. There are points of my childhood which I wish never would've happened or could be erased forever. Too bad there is no "eraser" for that.

As parents normally do when they have little ones, they hire a babysitter when they go away to work or even to have their own "alone" time with each other or with their friends. In our case, we had lots of babysitters because on top of having jobs, my parents also owned a business. Many people watched us over the years such as neighbors, my aunts and my female cousins, my older male cousin, and Lord knows who else.

One particular evening, my parents had my older male cousin watch us and of course his younger brother came along. It was just the five of us, my 2 cousins, my sister, my brother, and I. After my parents left we had fun watching TV and doing the usual things kids do such as playing board games, dolls, or whatever else we found to entertain ourselves. My cousin was about 4 years older than I was so at the time he was around 17 or 18 years old and I was 13 or 14.

Around 9:00 p.m., he sent everyone to bed – except for me. He said that because I was the oldest, I could stay up late and watch TV with him. My brother and sister went upstairs to sleep in their beds while my younger cousin was in the same room with us but sleeping in a sleeping bag behind the couch facing away from the television.

The show my older cousin put on the television after everyone went to bed (although I don't remember the title of it) included several women running around in bikinis or topless. I sat down to watch it as well but I remember feeling uncomfortable because I am not normally allowed to watch those types of shows.

My older cousin was sitting on the floor watching the movie and I was sitting in a chair. At some point during the movie, I realized that my older cousin was slowly inching his way towards me. I was beginning to feel awkward at first but I tried to ignore him and concentrate on the movie. It wasn't until about ten minutes or more later that my attention went back on him. While I had my attention fully on the movie, he had managed to slide down the floor to where I was sitting. He was now sitting below me on the floor with his back leaned up against my chair. I was caught up in the movie so I wasn't really paying attention to him but at this point he had somehow managed to unbutton my blouse. My focus was turned back to him when I realized that he had his hand under my shirt and was playing with my nipple. I tried to move away from him but he just followed me to wherever I went.

Suddenly my younger cousin began to talk to us so I instantly pulled myself away. I told both of my cousins that I was tired and was going to bed and ran upstairs to my bedroom. When I got in my room, I put my pajamas on and crawled into bed. I couldn't sleep though. I lay awake staring at the ceiling for several hours waiting for mom and dad to come home.

What would they say? Should I tell them? Would my cousin get into trouble? Did my younger cousin see anything? I was embarrassed. I was surprised. To be honest, I didn't know what to think. Did that movie just make him horny? Why would he try something like that with me? That never happened before. Is it normal for cousins to do that? My older cousin was very cute and

I sometimes wished we weren't related. Did he think I was cute too? Granted all he did was "touch" me. Was that even wrong? He didn't force me to do things. I guess it could've been worse. Thank God it wasn't.

As I lay there thinking about it, I came to the conclusion that maybe it was not that big of a deal. I mean, come on – we didn't have sex. He just touched my boob. I am sure that cousins have "experimented" with their cousins before, right? There is a curiosity factor in there, isn't there? Besides, it's not like he did it for very long. I did get out of there right away before anything else happened. That should be okay, right?

I don't know. To be honest, I was half expecting my cousin to follow me or say something. I even thought he would try to stop me from going upstairs but he didn't. He must have not wanted to push the issue further. I can't say. I am thankful that he didn't though. I was just glad that it was over. So how come I can't sleep? Why is it bothering me?

After lying in bed for several hours and thinking it over, I decided that it is best for everyone to just forget it ever happened. I didn't want to get my cousin into trouble and my mother wouldn't probably believe me anyway. I just didn't want this to turn into a major catastrophe. It wasn't that big of a deal. All he did was touch me. It was over now. Just forget about it.

I can say though that I never really forgot about it. Even now, as I'm telling this story, I am wondering if there are things I should've done to avoid that situation. As innocent as the "touch" might have been, he did still violate me in some fashion. Just like Amy did. Only in my cousin's case, he didn't use threats or force. He used sneakiness. I didn't even know he was there. I was too engrossed in a stupid movie.

I kept blaming myself afterwards. I shouldn't have watched the movie at all. I should have just gone to bed when my brother and sister did. The previous event from when I was younger was still with me and this new event caused me to struggle with my emotions. I was beginning to feel very self-conscious and unsure of myself. I started to doubt myself with people and began to lose faith and trust in anyone.

How can a person honestly be that stupid to just get so enthralled in a movie that they don't pay attention to someone taking advantage of them? I mean, come on! Seriously! It may have been "no big deal" but emotionally, it was a big deal to me. I felt violated again. I felt used. I tried to let it go but I couldn't. I kept playing the scenario over and over again in my mind. I began to wonder about the "What If's." What if I kept ignoring him? Would he have kept going? Would he have undressed me completely? What if I yelled? Would my other cousin defend me? I was driving myself crazy. My mind just wouldn't let it go.

I promised myself though that I wouldn't tell on him. I didn't want to get him or me into any trouble. I mean I was up late after all. I would probably get in trouble for that anyway. I was positive at the time that somehow it would get turned back on me if I did say anything. Even though he touched me, I am sure for some reason or another, it would be my fault for something. All I could do was bury it down deep with the other incident and try to forget about everything. I just wish actually doing so was easy.

CHAPTER 4

More Pain In High School

The rest of my school days were a blur – that is of course except for high school. High school was the worst time of my life. It was the time when my life just seemed to fall apart around me. My grades were alright but everything else struggled. I didn't realize it at the time but I was very emotionally unstable. I never really understood what the impact of those past events had on me. I just tried to forget what had happened and refused to think about them. Unfortunately, they were always on my mind. I think that was the worst thing I could have ever done.

I remember closing myself off to everyone. I would spend every evening locked up in my bedroom. My mother would "bark" at me to do chores but I would just ignore her until she would come up the stairs and yell at me. For the most part, I just wanted to be left alone. I was the happiest alone in my room listening to music.

I started to realize that I had a problem with relationships in high school. I had trouble keeping friends and my relationships with boys never lasted very long. I remember crying all of the time for no reason and getting angry at the slightest drop of a hat. When I did find boyfriends that would stay with me, they would touch me inappropriately or make innuendos regarding sex. I had a hard time telling them no so for the most part; I would just break up with them as soon as they turned our relationship sexual. I was never really taught the appropriate thing to do or say in that situation so I felt in my mind; it was the right thing to do.

I remember one boy that I dated. He was very popular in school. He played the trombone and made friends with boys in different grades besides his own. He was a grade under me but I thought he was cute. We dated for only about a week. Our band class went on a field trip to a musical and on the bus on the way home he put his hand down my underwear. When we stopped for lunch, I begged my friend to help me. I told her what he was doing and I asked her to help me get away from him. She seemed hesitant to help me. When he got back on the bus, he "demanded" that I get back in the seat beside him. When I said no, he threatened me so I reluctantly sat down. He then proceeded to pick up where he left off.

When we arrived back at the school, I was scared and angry with him. I didn't know what else to do so I broke up with him. I found out later that he didn't like that and apparently spread a rumor around school that I was "easy" or a "slut." From that point on, I became the laughing stock at school. I began to lose all of my friends and no boys would date me – at least seriously. The ones that did only did so because they thought I was an "easy lay."

My self-esteem began to fall even farther. I began to suffer from depression and spent more time in my bedroom alone and crying than ever before.

I just wanted to find a boy or even a friend that would care about me for who I was on the inside. I felt like all I received at home was yelling. My sister and I would fight all of the time. My father was always working and when my mother was home, she would yell at me for not doing chores or not having better grades. I rarely saw any affection from family members. They showed affection through "stuff." They would buy me expensive things to show they cared but I just wanted them to talk to me or give me a hug. The few times I tried to talk to my mother about my feelings, she would be watching TV at the same time and I felt ignored. I remember one time she and I were fighting, she said that I "needed to stay in my bedroom and don't come out until I'm twenty-one!" She thought I was just a hormonal teenager.

I remember one day during all of this going on that we went to my aunt's house so she could babysit us. She has four kids (my cousins) of her own that are roughly the same age as my brother, sister, and I. We grew up together and had a lot of fun together laughing and playing as kids do. I remember having a bad spell of depression while I was there and my aunt confronted me about it. I finally broke down and told her about my past. She instantly grew sympathetic and tried to comfort me. She told me that she was going to tell my mother everything. I instantly became upset and begged her not to. She reassured me that my mom would believe me and do something about it. I disagreed with her but she kept reassuring me that everything was going to be okay.

The next day, my aunt and I went to talk to my mother. She and I told her what had happened with my other cousin. I couldn't tell her what happened at the other school though. My mom didn't believe me at first but when I reassured her, she said that she would talk to my uncle about it. About a week later, my mother told me that my cousin denied everything. My mother believed him and said that I shouldn't make up stories. From that point on I decided that I would never tell anyone anything ever again. It was clear to me that no one would believe me anyway. They only thought I said those things to get attention. The only person I could trust was myself. No one cared whether I lived or died – at least that is what I thought.

As you can imagine, the remaining school years were the same as previously mentioned – if not worse. I went in and out of relationships with friends and boyfriends. I couldn't really trust either one – my friends or my boyfriends. I felt that everyone was out to hurt me and no one cared about me at all. I felt the happiest when I was alone. The few times that I did try to open up with friends, they ended up flirting with my boyfriends, getting my boyfriends to break up with me so they can date them, or use me for rides, money, etc.

As happy as I thought I was being alone, I can honestly say that I was more miserable. My depression grew intensely worse and I lost the desire to want to live. I began to pray to God that He would give me illnesses so that I would just die.

He actually answered my prayers. My health did begin to deteriorate – physically, emotionally, and spiritually. I started having problems with pain in my body and kept going in and out of the emergency room. The doctors struggled finding the cause however. Because of this, my mother would always say that I was faking my health problems to get attention as well. I just started to give up on everything after that.

The event that REALLY put a "rift" between my mom and I was what happened on Christmas one year. I don't remember how old I was though. It became very clear to me at this point that she only thought badly of me.

We were at a family Christmas party out of town. I was in a bedroom playing cars with one of my cousins. We were looking for more cars to play with so I decided to open some doors in a dresser. I did not find any cars in there but I was shocked to find that there was a lot of cash inside. Just at this moment, the owner of the house walked by and told my mom what had happened. She punished me and made me apologize in front of everyone for stealing. I tried to tell her that I wasn't stealing anything. I came across the money by accident while looking for cars but she wouldn't believe me. She insisted that I was stealing and kept yelling at me. She refused to let me leave until I apologized. I just stared at her with such anger. I couldn't believe it. I finally gave in and apologized but deep down I resented her for that. I was forced to apologize for something I didn't even do. I realized at that moment that everyone thought the worst in me. No matter what I did, they would only think what a horrible person I was.

I remember I hit the lowest point of my life after that. My emotions were all over the place and I started to believe that maybe everyone was right about me. I was a horrible person and everyone hated me. I remember being in high school and literally hating myself. It was my junior year in high school and I started thinking of suicide a lot. My emotional pain was so deep and so strong that I began writing dark poems and wishing I was dead.

I remember one day my mom yelled at me to do dishes. I fought her at first but eventually went into the kitchen. I walked into the kitchen and saw all of the dirty dishes on the counter and lost all hope in living. I felt like my life was nothing more than playing the cleaning lady and that is all people wanted me around for. No one cared about me. No one would even miss me if I wasn't around.

When I went into the kitchen, I saw a really large knife on the counter and I picked it up. I put it to my left wrist and began to cut my wrist. As it started to cut the skin and blood began to drip down, I heard a voice say "NO!" I was startled and dropped the knife to the floor. I picked up a towel that was close by and wiped the blood up and looked around for the source of the voice but no one was there. I began to realize that the voice I had heard was God's voice. He told me to stop. I picked up the knife off of the floor and whispered to Him, "I am sorry Lord." I then began to wash the dishes.

My senior year of high school began to change. I tried to get more involved in the artistic classes and I found joy in singing, music, writing, and art. I finally found an outlet for my pain. I even met a boy that I truly fell in love with. I thought my life was slowly beginning to turn around. He was so sweet and would tell me how beautiful and smart I was. His words began to uplift my spirit and I wanted to talk to him all of the time. Just talking to him or being with him would stop my depression. He made me so happy. I even started to think good things of myself again. I found one person on the whole entire planet that actually cared about me!

After we had been dating for quite some time, I decided that I was ready to have sex. I was still a virgin at this point but I wanted to give up my virginity to him. I felt that we were in love and we would be together forever. I finally found love. We had made plans to go to a party together that night and I thought this would be the perfect time.

Unfortunately, when I got to the party I couldn't find him anywhere. I asked my friends where he might be and no one knew. About a few hours later, someone told me that he was in town at another girl's house. I asked them what they meant by that. They said that he was having sex with a girl and would not be at the party until much later. I was devastated. I couldn't believe what they told me. They had to be lying! He wouldn't do that to me! Would he?

About an hour later, he finally showed up to the party. I instantly confronted him about what I was told. He said that he was in town and there were girls there but he didn't have sex with any of them. He was just with some friends and he apologized for worrying me. I was still angry with him but I slowly understood and forgave him. He used his sweet words and slowly won me over.

We began to kiss alone in the woods outside of the party and then I went ahead and let him make love to me. It was very painful and he felt so bad for hurting me but I told him that it was okay because I was still a virgin and I heard the first time was painful. I don't think he knew I was a virgin because he seemed shocked by this. He didn't talk to me the rest of the evening. He just stared out the window of the car and we then went our separate ways.

About a week or two following this event, I received a telephone call from a girl at our school. She proceeded to tell me that she found out that he and I were boyfriend and girlfriend and I confirmed that what she was told was correct. She became upset and told me that she and he also were "going steady."

"What?!" I asked shockingly.

"He told me that you are both boyfriend and girlfriend. Well he and I are boyfriend and girlfriend too!" She replied.

"Oh….." was all I could say.

"In fact, I hear he has two other girlfriends also besides us!" She replied.

I instantly became quiet and depressed. This had happened just a few days before I had given up my virginity to him. I was saving it for someone special. I thought it was him. Now I am hearing this. I didn't know what to think. Could she be lying to me just to have him for herself like my other friends have done in the past? What if it's true? I began to feel devastated and betrayed.

"Okay. Thank you for letting me know." I answered quietly and then hung up.

I instantly called him on the telephone and told him what the girl had said. He eventually admitted everything saying it was all true. I became angry on the telephone and asked him why he would do this to me. He didn't respond. I told him we were over.

For about a month or two after that, he continued to beg me to take him back. I kept telling him to get lost. He kept apologizing and stating that he will never do that again. After about a month or so of begging, I finally gave in and took him back. It was the worst mistake I could have made because shortly after I took him back, I got the exact same telephone call from that same girl. He was four-timing me again! I instantly broke up with him again and once again, he begged me to take him back – which I of course, stupidly did. This process went on at least 3 or 4 times. To this day, I still do not know why I believed his lies. I shouldn't have taken him back the second time let alone the third or fourth time!

The final time I broke up with him was at a basketball game at our high school. I had gone to the game to meet him there in the hopes of spending some time with him but unfortunately I couldn't find him anywhere. I left the game and proceeded to walk around the school. It wasn't until I reached the parking lot that I found him. He was making out with another girl in his car. I knocked on the window. When he saw me, he was shocked and asked what I was doing there. I told him that he was an asshole and we were officially over for good this time. He tried to chase me but I told him to stay away from me and never talk to me again.

For me, that was the final straw that broke the camels' back you could say. I instantly fell apart. The only person that I actually began to trust cheated on me several times! It became clear to me that I would never be able to trust anyone ever again! I felt that everyone was out to hurt me in some fashion. I lost all hope at that moment in people and in anything. I quite literally wanted to just give up and die.

CHAPTER 5

Glimpse Of Hope And Further Devastation

That night, I had no rational thinking. All I thought about was the pain and how I didn't want to feel it anymore. The only peace I found was in the moon. I decided that I would sit in the middle of the school driveway and wait for a car to hit me while I stared peacefully at the moon. I knew that it meant physical pain and maybe even death but at that moment, I didn't care and I didn't want to live anymore. I was ready to go. I was ready for the pain to stop.

I didn't sit there very long; however, when a car pulled up beside me and out came one of my friends.

"What are you doing in the middle of the road?" She asked shockingly.

"Waiting for a car to hit me." Was all I could say.

"Why?" She asked.

"My boyfriend cheated on me again and I am ready to die." I told her while I stared at the moon.

"I am not leaving you like this. Get in the car with me!" She demanded.

"Are there boys in there?" I asked angrily.

"Yes. My boyfriend and his friend." She answered.

"Then hell no! I am not getting in the car with any boy!"

"I am not leaving you in the middle of the street!"

"I am not going!"

"Get in the car!"

At that moment, she began dragging my arm and forcing me into the car. Reluctantly, I got into the passenger seat next to her boyfriend's friend while she and her boyfriend sat in the back seat. We drove around town for a while. All I could do was hold on tightly to the door handle. I waited patiently for a chance to get out of the car. I didn't want to be there – especially around more boys. I just wanted to be alone.

We drove to an abandoned parking lot and the driver decided to break the ice a bit. He drove the car in donuts and made all of us scream! I have to admit that it made me smile and laugh. After that, I no longer remembered why I was hurting.

33

From there we all decided to park the car at a local park. The driver and I got out and talked while my friend and her boyfriend stayed in the car making out. I was scared being with him and didn't trust him yet. I thought he was nice though and tried to at least give him a chance. We got to know each other and he showed me a poem that he got published. I read his poem and instantly my heart softened for him. I thought it was the sweetest thing.

It was actually a blessing though. That one encounter made me forget all about what happened with my boyfriend. I was surprised to find that I was slowly becoming attracted to this new guy but part of me was so scared. I didn't want this new guy to treat me poorly too and I was so tired of crying. I was interested in him but did my best to keep a distance. I had to protect myself for a change. I thought it was so cool though because my friend had brought us together. If I hadn't gotten in that car, we would have never met. I could have also been hit by a car and could be dead by now. She saved my life – in more ways than one! I now know that God intervened here like He did in my kitchen. Just like He stopped me from slitting my wrists, here He forced me into the car and forced me to meet this guy. He saved my life a second time!

As the days went by, the driver and I drew closer. He attended the local vocational center to study welding. I often would meet him at the front of the school before he left just to talk and to get to know him better. My friend kept pressuring me to ask him out but I kept telling her that he had to ask me. I couldn't tell if he was interested in me or anything and I didn't want him to think what everyone else did – that I was "easy." I wanted him to like me for me!

Finally after weeks of pressuring me, I finally gave in and just wrote him a letter. I told him that I did like him and if he was interested in me, he could ask me out and I would say yes. Apparently that letter made him happy because he asked me on a date right after I gave him the letter. Our first date together wasn't anything special (just a movie and McDonald's) but to me it was. We had so much fun and I fell in love with how much he made me laugh.

As the days went on, we grew closer. I started to feel so overwhelmed with emotion for him. I started to feel sad when we weren't together. I felt like I was under some kind of spell or drug. I couldn't get enough of him and longed to just talk to him every day. We started growing more serious and became boyfriend and girlfriend and stayed that way all through the senior year of high school. It was the happiest year of my life! I was so sad when high school was over because I knew college was coming and I wasn't sure how our relationship would continue. Would we stay together as boyfriend and girlfriend? Would we survive a long-distance relationship? Would we get married? I wanted to ask him but I was so scared. I didn't want to scare him away.

We eventually talked about it and we agreed to stay together. He was willing to visit me on a regular basis and we would always call and write each other. I felt content with that and tried not to pursue the issue any further.

Unfortunately, other people did not approve of us being together. I kept receiving pressure from family and other people to break up with him. They wanted me to keep dating and not settle down yet. They kept telling me that I would meet a lot of nice boys in college and that I should try it. I kept arguing with them and telling them that I didn't want to date anyone else. It wasn't until they told me that I was being unfair to my boyfriend and I was hurting him, that I started to listen. I didn't want to make my boyfriend miserable by trying to make a long-distance relationship work. Maybe he would be happier with someone else. My self-esteem was still so low at this point that I honestly felt he would be happier without me, so before I left for college, I broke up with him. We both cried as we sat in the car talking about it. I honestly thought they were right. Maybe they weren't. I knew at that moment it was the biggest mistake of my life.

I tried to make it work though. I tried to keep up a smile and tried to follow family's advice but that feeling was confirmed in college. I even tried dating other guys several times. Each time I tried though, I kept comparing them to my now ex-boyfriend. They didn't talk like him or they didn't act like him, etc. I found something wrong with every single one of them. I would spend my nights at college while everyone else was partying, crying in my dorm room. I was so alone and so unhappy. All I wanted to do was go back home and try to win him back. I was so afraid that I lost him forever. I was afraid that he had found someone new and didn't want me back.

If that wasn't bad enough, the guys I did date hurt me even more. One guy I dated had a great personality. He invited me to his family's house for Thanksgiving one year and I got to get to know him and his family well, especially his little sister. She and I became close. I started to feel a little comfortable with him but I still had feelings for my ex. I was trying to let my ex from home "move on" though so I decided to try too.

One night this new guy and I decided to go see a movie. We stopped by his dorm room so he could change and he gave me a glass of wine. As I looked out the window drinking the wine, I thought about how beautiful it was there. The moon shone so bright and it was nice to be in college. I can honestly say that it was the last thing I remember. The next day I found myself naked on his dorm room floor covered by a blanket! I don't know what happened between the moment with the moon and the night before. He must have drugged my wine! I had never had that happen to me before! I was so scared and mortified! I didn't know what to do! Do I call the police? I was so ashamed!

"Did we . . .?" I asked him shaking.

"Yep!" He replied with a smile.

Following this event, he kept stalking me. He would make me music tapes, call me, meet me at my dorm, etc. I did everything in my power to stay away from him. I was so scared of him! I am so thankful though that he didn't stalk me long. He ended up dating another girl in my dorm and ignored me after that. I was still close with his sister though. She would often send me letters and I started getting more scared of him every time I got one of her letters. I couldn't believe what she put in them! I was starting to see the "real" him! I am glad that I ended it with him when I did. I felt ashamed though. If only I knew all of this beforehand. I wouldn't have gone home with him for Thanksgiving. I wouldn't have even gone to his dorm room that night. I could do nothing but blame myself. Once again, I am so stupid.

My emotional state started to fall again. I was so ashamed of myself. I should have done more to stop him or I should have called the police after I realized what he had done. To be honest, I didn't realize he even drugged me until it was pointed out to me years later. I felt so naïve and stupid. I started suffering from depression again. I often stared into outerspace and didn't talk to anyone. My friends began to worry about me and they reported me to the college. The next thing I knew, the college started forcing me to attend counseling sessions and filling out questionnaires that were hundreds of pages long. The demands for these began to interfere with my classes. Between my emotional state and these questionnaires, my grades started to fall dramatically and I started to fear losing my scholarship. When family confronted me about it, I just lied and said that I was involved too much with band and hockey. They wouldn't understand the truth and even if they did, they would just think even worse of me than they already did. I couldn't handle the thought of that.

I tried to date again though. I met a nice guy that helped me with my homework and carry my books. He had a great sense of humor and he reminded me so much of a friend from back home. He also treated me to dinner a lot and he made me feel safe somehow. He never pressured me into sex or anything but honestly, I felt like he was more like a brother than a boyfriend.

I remember sitting on my bed with him one day watching a moving when my ex-boyfriend from back home called me. We talked for quite a while and it felt like we were still together! I was so happy because I began to realize that he truly did love me. It was confirmation that breaking up with him was a mistake. He wasn't happier without me! I began to feel awkward though because my current boyfriend was sitting on the bed next to me and my ex from home refused to let me get off the telephone until I told him that I loved him. What would my new boyfriend say if I did that? I felt torn between two guys! This has never happened before!

I couldn't deny the fact though that deep down I did still love my ex. I wanted so much to say those words to him and I knew I didn't love the new one. The new one was wonderful but he just felt more like a brother to me. I was so surprised though that my ex from home did this! I can't believe he loves me! I was so happy! I didn't ruin things with him after all! He's not happier without me! In fact, he kept saying how miserable he was without me and he refused to date anyone else! I had never dated a guy that cared so much and so deeply for me before. Have I finally found the "one?"

Well, what can a girl do? I said those three little words! My new boyfriend gave me a "look" and I couldn't say anything in response. What is there to say? I tried to explain things to him later and he seemed to understand. He finally agreed to remain as friends. He still treated me to dinner as friends once in a while and it was nice that things worked out well. I began to tell him all about my ex from home. I told him how we met and how long we were together. He never said anything but he seemed to be interested.

As the days went by, my ex from home and I made things official. We were finally back together as boyfriend and girlfriend. He even tried to visit me in college several times. I was around 300+ miles away from home so he would have to use his paycheck from work and visit me on the weekends. It was so wonderful to see him and hold him again! I showed him all of my favorite spots in college. I even showed him the beautiful waterfall and that became "our spot." Being with him again raised my spirits and I began to work hard again in my studies. My mood began to improve again and the depression was almost gone. I felt like a new person again.

My happiness was short-lived however. Unbeknownst to me, my college boyfriend that I broke up with was upset with me that I was back with my ex. He started acting weird and started demanding that I owed him sex. I told him no. I couldn't do that to my boyfriend. He just kept arguing with me. Hurt and angry, I just walked away. I couldn't believe it! We were supposed to be friends. Friends don't treat each other that way. Why was he acting this way? Was the only reason he was so nice with me was to get me into bed?! Why are people this way? Why does everyone I start to trust, treat me like this? My heart began to sink. I felt betrayed and used all over again. I started to lose faith in people again.

Shortly after this happened, I went to stay at a hotel for a night so I could study for the big exam coming up. I wanted to do well on my test and it was hard to study with so many people around making so much noise. While I was there studying, my college ex-boyfriend showed up and told me to take a break and go swimming with him. I finally gave in because I wanted to swim at least once while I was there and I needed a break. When we were done swimming, we both went back up to my hotel room and he helped me study and he cheered me up by making me laugh. It felt like we were friends again and I tried to forget about our earlier argument. I just tried to have fun and worry about the exam.

Later that evening, we decided to take a break from studying and watch a movie so we turned on the television and began watching a movie. He sat on one bed and I laid on my belly on the other. We watched the movie for quite a while not talking when I suddenly noticed that my ex had managed to move over to my side of the room and was sitting beside me on my bed. It was only a few minutes after realizing this when he had jumped on top of me in the hotel room and was taking my clothes off. Needless to say, he got what he was truly after.

He ended up staying there in the hotel room with me the entire night and when checkout came the next morning, we both walked together back to the campus. I can honestly say that the whole

41

walk back to college was a nightmare. I couldn't even stand next to him. I was so disgusted. I didn't want anything to do with him anymore. It was obvious to me that he just used me like everyone else I ever trusted. Our relationship as boyfriend and girlfriend and even friendship was officially over. I told my boyfriend from home all that had happened. I kept apologizing to him. I felt so ashamed. I should have done more to stop him. Once again, I blamed myself.

I also told him about the first boyfriend and the drug in the wine. He was so understanding and compassionate towards me. I felt like I didn't deserve his love. In a way, I wanted him to hate me. It was what I deserved but he just kept saying how much he loved me and forgave me. He then started to get angry and began threatening to beat up both of the other guys. I made him promise not to because I didn't want him arrested or anything. I also didn't want him to because I felt like it was my fault – not theirs. I don't know why I blamed myself. I guess I shouldn't have but all I kept thinking about was what I could have done differently. I felt unworthy of his love. All I wanted was for both of us to forget what happened and move on. I honestly don't think either of us could, however.

He reluctantly agreed not to hurt them and we worked hard getting our relationship back together. He would drive up practically every other weekend just so we could spend more time together. We always had so much fun together and yes, we often made love.

I remember feeling down and depressed one night while he was visiting me. I still felt so ashamed of myself for everything and thought that maybe he should let me go. I began crying and we argued. He was so upset with me but instead of saying anything mean to me or agreeing with me about leaving me, he proposed to me! I was so taken back that I couldn't do anything but say yes and cry! He still loved me after everything that happened. I was so happy and it proved to me just how much he did love me. He wants to spend his entire life with me! I began to feel anxious for college to end so we could spend our life together.

Even though I was happy at this point however, my grades started to drop even further and I eventually lost my financial aid. I was forced to leave college and return home with no college degree. I was so devastated but at the same time I was very happy because I knew that he and I could now get married and be together forever. This time, there wouldn't be college or family that could stand in our way.

PART 2

HOW I FOUND HOPE

CHAPTER 6

My Salvation

It was around 1993 to 1994 when I was away in college living in a dorm. Because of my grades and losing my scholarship and financial aid, I was forced to only attend college for about a year and a half. It was the fall or winter of 1994 when I came back home to live with my parents.

After about a month of living with my parents, they informed me that they would be moving back to the town I grew up in as a child – the town that I had so happily left. Devastated, I talked things over with my fiancé and told him that we had to do something. I didn't want to go back there again and be around those memories. I didn't want to feel the horror I felt from before. I just wanted to stay here with him.

After much deliberating, he eventually told me that he and I could live with his grandparents. They are both on the road a lot being semi drivers so we would be basically watching their house for them while they were gone. I discussed this with my parents and I was shocked to find that they didn't argue. They basically said I was an adult now and they couldn't stop me. I was so happy. He and I would be living together!

We lived with his grandparents for a short while and later moved in with his mother. We lived with her for a few more months while we worked on saving money and keeping steady jobs. In 1995, we eventually got a small apartment together. It was wonderful being on our own. My only complaint was that the water there was so rusty. It often left the water orange colored and it tasted horrible to drink.

During this time, we were also hard at work planning our wedding. We both agreed that we wanted our wedding to be in May but struggled picking the right weekend. We eventually settled on May 25th. I remember arguing quite often with my mom during the planning stage. She and I often disagreed as to how the decorations and colors should go but we eventually settled on the perfect wedding. Our colors ended up being dark purple and white. We picked out beautiful fake flowers and one of my aunts agreed to sing at the wedding while my other aunt made the cake for us. It was turning out to be a beautiful wedding.

When May 25, 1996 finally arrived, I was so overcome with emotion. I was so busy with the planning that I really didn't have time to let the events sink in. Everything was so beautiful but it was happening. It was really happening! I am getting married! Oh my gosh! I couldn't believe that this day was finally here! I had convinced myself that no one would ever love me and I would be alone forever. I never thought in a million years that I would actually get married! It is definitely a miracle! I couldn't imagine ever being as happy as I was at this moment! Thank you Lord! Not only did You save me twice, but You brought us together! The wedding was so beautiful. Everything turned out wonderful and on top of that, we were married in a Catholic church. It just felt like everything was going right for the first time in my life.

I didn't know this at the time, but my husband was a Christian. I honestly didn't know what that meant. I was always raised as a Catholic and was baptized as a baby but really didn't understand anything about Christianity or being "saved." The only thing that I was sure of was that I knew God existed and I wanted to get married in a Catholic church. To be honest, I had never visited any other churches beside Catholic churches so I really didn't know anything about other religions or beliefs either. I just wanted to marry in a church before God. To me, that was the most important thing.

After about three years of marriage in 1999, my husband started trying to talk me into going to church with him. He attended a small church in town but it was Pentecostal, not Catholic. Every time he asked though, I would tell him no. Finally, after much pestering on his part, I agreed to go to church with him. At the time, they had their services in a small theatre. They were a very small congregation and were still building their church family. It was actually a very nice church. The people there were so friendly and it felt great to not be around too many people that I didn't know.

I have to admit though, that I felt a little awkward at first. I was always raised Catholic growing up. I believed in God and knew He existed, but my family never attended church regularly. I just felt in my heart that He existed and I knew it was His voice when He would speak to me. At this church, I felt more of a "tug" from Him than ever before. I never really understood the difference between Catholics and Pentecostals. I did notice that the Pentecostals were more outgoing in their praises to Him. I struggled at first following along with the services but I felt more alive. I began feeling joy in my heart again and when the pastor said a prayer for non-believers, I decided to say it as well. On that day, I asked Jesus into my heart. I was so excited. I knew at that moment that I would never be the same. For the first time in my file, I finally understood what it meant to be "saved." My rebirth was in October of 1999.

The most exciting event that happened to me while I was attending this church however occurred towards the beginning of my attendance. To this day, I am still amazed at how quickly the Lord worked on my heart. As I stated earlier, I have always been raised in a Catholic home. Although we didn't always attend church on Sundays, we still tried to follow Catholic traditions and rules. We also recited the Lord's Prayer at meals. I was told that as a Catholic, I was baptized as a baby and I also remember as a child partaking of my First Communion. I remember wearing a little white dress and to this day, I still have my First Communion candle.

At the Pentecostal church with my husband, the pastor one Sunday began doing a service regarding baptism. I didn't pay too much attention to it because I knew I was already baptized as a baby. I stood with everyone else and looked around at the other people but didn't really pay attention to what the pastor was saying. Suddenly, he began calling people up to the altar to be baptized. I started to sit down thinking that this wasn't for me when all of a sudden I heard a loud audible voice in my ear.

"GO!" It said.

"What?" I asked.

"GO!" It said again.

After contemplating the word for a minute, I suddenly realized that I was hearing the voice of God again. He was telling me to go to the altar.

As all humans do, I began to argue with Him.

"I've already been baptized, Lord!" I whispered back to Him.

He didn't respond but instead tugged at my heart to walk to the front. Hesitantly, I forced myself slowly to the front of the room. The pastor put his hand on the top of my head and began praying over me. I bowed my head and closed my eyes. I felt another woman come over and she also put her hands on my shoulders and began praying over me also.

I started to feel awkward. This didn't seem right. Don't you get baptized in water? I didn't understand what was happening. What were they doing? Why were they praying over me? All I could do was keep my eyes closed and pray to God. I started to talk to Him. I asked that He change my life and bless my marriage. I prayed for family members to be saved. I prayed for the blessing of children. I just kept talking to Him about anything and everything. After several minutes my words began to turn into worship to Him. I started saying "Hallelujah" over and over to Him. After doing this for several minutes, I began to feel light headed and I started to shake from head to foot. My words of "Hallelujah" slowly became gibberish. My words were not understandable. I didn't understand what was happening. I didn't know what I was saying. I began crying hysterically and shaking uncontrollably. I didn't know what was going on.

"Oh my gosh! What just happened?" I asked the woman.

"You were just baptized in the Holy Spirit. Doesn't it feel wonderful?" She replied.

All I could do was shake my head yes. She gave me a hug and I cried hard on her shoulder. It was the most exciting experience of my life. It was an experience that I had never felt before. As a Catholic we had always prayed to a cross with Jesus on it or to the Virgin Mary. We always recited the same old prayers and talked about Jesus' sacrifice on the cross. I never felt Him before – at least not like that! I have always believed in Him but never felt Him – at least not in that powerful of a way before. I was also excited because I heard His voice again! He told me to go and I went! I could not deny His existence anymore!

It was at that moment that I realized how true and real He is. It was at that moment that made me want to be closer to Him. My entire life changed after that moment. When I got home, I went through all of my music and threw away anything that I thought might be offensive to Him. I went through movies I owned and gave away things that were too violent or sexual. I stopped swearing. I started doing Bible studies. I did everything in my power to spend more time with Him. I wanted to be closer to Him. I wanted to feel that wonderful power of His all of the time.

For the first time in my entire life I felt so much joy and happiness. For so many years I have felt nothing but pain. All I had ever done was cry. I didn't like to smile. I didn't laugh at all. All I did was go through the motions and do my best to avoid people. I was like a robot. I never showed emotions to others. I always kept everything bottled up inside of me. It was when I was alone, that I cried myself to sleep.

Feeling His power that day opened up a new door for me. I began to see that there was in fact hope after all. I was so excited for Him and His presence that I wanted that all of the time. It was much more enjoyable than all of the pain I normally felt. I felt peace and happiness. I also felt that someone actually loved me – REALLY loved ME and it was God! He gave His life for me. No one has ever done that for me. It just made my heart sing. All I could do was weep for joy. I had never cried happy tears before.

It's now 2022 and as I look back on that moment, I am overwhelmed. Since that moment, He has done so many wonderful things for me. He has really taught me so many things and I would have never imagined being where I am at this moment in my life. I am still daily striving to be near Him. I am still attending a Pentecostal church.

I can say that I have been baptized twice. I was baptized in water and I was baptized in the Holy Spirit. The Baptism of the Holy Spirit was evidenced by when I "spoke in tongues." Since that baptism, I speak in tongues every time I pray to Him. God has even used me to speak in tongues during services – to give messages to His congregation out loud. When this occurs, I speak in tongues out loud and then another person will interpret out loud what I have said. It's truly amazing to be used in this way by Him. I feel so overwhelmed by His spirit when He touches me.

I have also prayed for other gifts of His such as the gift of interpretation and prophesy. I just love to be serving Him in this way. I constantly want more of Him every day. I would love to be able to be used by Him to help people and reach people as He has done for me.

One Sunday morning during service, He granted me another gift. I was so surprised. He tugged at my heart as usual to give a message in tongues so I began speaking out loud and He took over. When it was over, I waited as usual for the interpretation but it didn't come. I was confused but then He kept saying to me "children" over and over. I finally said children out loud and once again, He took over. He used me to give tongues to the congregation and then again to give the interpretation! I was shaking so hard after that event! I felt so honored and excited! Praises be to Him! He blessed me with another gift!

I have to admit that I would have never imagined myself to know God in this way. I never thought that you could feel Him like this, let alone be blessed with such amazing gifts by Him. I didn't even know about this type of service to the Lord. The Catholics never taught this! I would not have ever known about His great gifts or power if my husband hadn't coaxed me into his church. I feel so blessed. I feel so much love and happiness. With His Holy Spirit inside of me, I feel love, hope, and joy where there used to be pain, death, and despair. I feel like a new person. I feel like I have been reborn.

CHAPTER 7

The Learning Stage

For so many years, I was in a dark place. My thoughts and focus were on dark things. Granted I never thought of "evil" things such as murder, etc. but at the same time, they were on hopelessness and pain. I thought I was destined to be miserable. I thought I would be alone forever and that everyone would hate me. I had no hope or faith in anything. Every time someone would try to cheer me up or give me positive things to think on, I would reject them or their words. It sounded too good to be true – at least for me. They were allowed to be happy but I wasn't.

I also had no control over my life. I felt like everyone around me was telling me what to do, guiding my path, or not allowing me to choose what I wanted. I didn't know what my likes or dislikes were. Every time I tried to make a choice, someone would tell me "no." I began to give up. I stopped choosing anything for myself. What's the point? No one would let me have it anyway.

When I started going to counseling while married, my counselor told my husband to force me to make choices. He started out small like forcing me to pick out a movie at a movie theater. I was shocked! Not shocked that he let me pick a movie but more shocked that he didn't say no when I did! I had always been told no! From there, I started to figure out who I really was and what things I liked.

I slowly began to feel like a person and not just a robot! I learned that my favorite color is purple! My favorite food is barbecue chicken and I love to watch hockey! I would not have known that otherwise. I just took what people gave me – did what people told me to do. It was an amazing feeling to finally learn after twenty years or more that I do have likes and dislikes. I was a real person and my husband also cared about me and what made me happy!

My Christian walk has been so uplifting. I have learned so many things about God as well as myself. Granted I am still going through counseling but I am so much better now than where I used to be. I give God all of the credit. Yes counseling got me talking about my problems but He was the one who truly healed me! He healed my heart and in some ways, He has also healed my body!

As I think over what I went through in my past, I am amazed that I didn't respond differently. Yes I have the "what if's" all of the time but I could've went in a different direction. I could've gone through with the suicide attempt. I could've become violent towards those I love. I could've done so many more evil things but He kept me from all of those things. He knew the pain I felt and

He stayed by my side through it all. When the time was right, He drew me closer to Him so that I could heal!

Over the past three years as He was teaching me about thoughts and focus, I began to learn that even though I was better, I was still thinking wrong. I was dwelling on that emotional pain from the past and allowing it to keep me down. I could never be fully healed until I changed my thoughts and focus.

The first thing I knew I had to do was tell someone about my past. Yes I saw counselors for the first ten years I was married but not once in those sessions did I tell anyone about Amy or Becky or what happened at the school. I kept all of those things buried. I don't know why. I think maybe part of me was still scared of what people would say or think about me but I didn't understand why. It's not like I had seen her since that day I left the school. She may not even be in the area anymore!

I think most of my struggle was that I was ashamed of myself. I knew that if I said those words out loud, people would judge me. They would say I was a pervert for doing those things or that I was gay. They would believe the lies that Amy and Becky spread and it would turn everyone away from me. I already had a school hate me and call me a pervert. I didn't want my husband to think that way of me too. I didn't want my family to disown me. I didn't want to be truly alone forever.

I felt so horrible about myself. I couldn't stand to look at myself in the mirror. No matter how hard I tried to make myself pretty,

I still felt ugly and disgusting. I couldn't stand the thought of others thinking worse of me than I already did. I would give up on life even more if my husband ever left me, especially if I knew he thought of me the way I did.

Now that I am a Christian, my thoughts of myself are beginning to change. I can actually look at myself in the mirror without cringing! I know that God loves me and He loves me in spite of all of that other stuff. He was there with me through it all. He saw what happened. He was with me afterwards too to keep me from hurting myself. Even if my family hated me or my husband hated me, I know He will never hate me. I am loved – even if it is only by Him!

I am trying so hard even now to love myself as He loves me but I admit that there are still days that I struggle with that. Every time I make a mistake, I think back to those days and feel like the "old me." I have to fight hard not to let that way break loose again. I have to keep telling myself that I am born again. I am not that person anymore. I need to remember what He did for me and that even in those mistakes, He loves me.

My counselor keeps telling me that I am the victim. It's not my fault. I try to agree with her when she says that but I often question if she's right. Would others see me as the victim if they truly knew what happened or would they think I am the pervert that Becky said? My heart is so fragile. I don't feel strong enough to take that kind of rejection. Yes I feel stronger than before but even now I wonder if I can deal with the ridicule of other people. It's all I have ever known.

I have never had any real friends. Every time I tried to make friends even in new places, my trust and faith in them hangs by a thread. They could have been perfect friends but I wouldn't let them in. If they even did one little thing to hurt me, I cut them loose. I didn't want to take the chance that they would laugh at me or make fun of me if I opened up to them. There's too much risk. I can handle being sick. I can handle health problems but I will never be able to handle going through that rejection all over again. It's too painful. Emotional pain is too strong.

CHAPTER 8

The Lord's Work In Me

Over the past eighteen years or more of "transformation" trying to walk the Christian walk, I have learned a lot of lessons. I have learned so much about forgiveness and faith. I have even learned to love myself. I will admit that I still have far to go and that journey probably will take a lifetime! One thing that will always stay with me though is that no matter where life leads me, I need to stay close to Him. Every time I stray too far from Him, the enemy brings those negative things back into my life. It's like a constant reminder of the pain and it tries to continuously draw me back in.

As long as I stay close to Him though, I gradually become stronger to resist those thoughts and feelings. It is a daily battle and I find myself continuously going back and forth. I find something "worldly" that seems pleasing to the eye and it sucks me back in. I then have to repent of it and try to come back.

In 2014 I had bariatric surgery on my stomach to lose weight. I weighed over 325 pounds and was suffering with so many health problems. My health problems got so severe that I was seeing a liver specialist. My liver was not doing well at all. The specialist finally pulled me aside in his office and told me that if I didn't have the surgery, I had only five years to live. I was devastated. I was finally saved and beginning to enjoy life and now it was going to end!

Researching the surgery didn't seem pleasing to me though. There were so many things that had to change in my daily routine and I was not strong enough to put myself through it. I wanted to be stronger emotionally before I endured that kind of procedure. It required a major diet change. It required constant medicine and vitamins. Yes my life was important and I should do all I could do to prolong it but at the same time I was unwilling to give up certain foods or take the steps necessary to follow the doctor's instructions.

My other fear factor was that there were always risks with that type of surgery and I heard of so many people who had problems afterwards. For many that had the procedure as well, their stomach stretched back out and they gained the weight back. I was afraid that I would put myself through all of it for nothing. It didn't help that family members did not agree and kept pushing the issue. One side of the family kept nagging me to do it while the other side kept encouraging me not to. I felt torn – like no one was on my side. They were just forcing me to do what they wanted again and they didn't care about how I felt about the topic. When I tried to share my opinion, they kept giving me guilt trips. Why won't they just leave me alone to make this decision myself?! Instead I would get: "think of your husband." As big as this decision was, I wanted to be the one to make it! Yes I knew that as husband and wife, we should make the decision together but at the same time, it was my body! I didn't want someone else to control me or make the decision for me.

After much discussion with my husband, I finally decided to go forward and have the procedure. To be honest, I gave in under the pressure. Deep down I really didn't want to go through with it at all. I even told my husband so. He said he wanted me to go through with it but he wouldn't force me to. I guess I got tired of the nagging and guilt trips. For years, I resented the decision and the people who pushed me into it. Eventually I began cutting myself down again though for even listening to them. I should have defended myself better. Why do I keep letting people manipulate me?

About four years after the surgery I began to change my attitude. I started to see the benefits of it and now I am glad that I did it. I have lost over one hundred pounds and many of the health problems are gone. It was a rough four years but I am better now and I don't even want to think about what would have happened had I not done the procedure at all. I admit though that it brought new health problems to the surface that I didn't even know were there. I guess you have to take the good with the bad though.

With regard to the new health problems, they became quite debilitating unfortunately. It was during this point where I was in a wheelchair for four years. My surgery was in April of 2014 and the new health problems began in August of 2014 and continued until 2018. Basically I found out during that period that my immune system is compromised and I have an autoimmune disease. I apparently had this problem before the surgery but the stress of the surgery progressed the disease. I may not have ever known I was that sick had it not been for the surgery though!

The reason for the wheelchair was caused by constant blackouts and dizzy spells. I was so dizzy that I could not walk without falling down and I would have three blackouts a day. I made numerous trips to the emergency room because my husband would come home from work and find me on the floor. I was always unable to get myself back up again. On top of that during my falls, I often would break bones and/or get a concussion so he would have to rush me to the emergency room. I sometimes hit my head on wooden bed frames or I would sprain or brake bones in my wrists or ankles. He was always scared that he would find me dead when he got home. He always hated leaving me home alone.

Thanks to the Lord though, the dizzy spells and blackouts have decreased in number. I am out of the wheelchair and can even drive a car again! I give God all of the praise and glory for my healing. I tried to listen to doctors for three out of four years and everything just seemed to get worse – not better. They were unsure of the causes and every test they did seemed to come back normal. I started to get frustrated and depressed. I began to give up on life again and often prayed that God would just take me home. I didn't want to suffer anymore.

The doctors tried to help but what they gave me only treated the symptoms like nausea and dizziness but none of it really helped me at all. I remember one day as I was lying on the sofa. I heard God speak to me again. He said: "You need to take charge of your own health. Stop trusting doctors." After that, I started doing research on my symptoms and found that a Candida infection can cause the problems I was struggling with. I began to do research online and found diets and treatments for the infection and decided it was worth a try. It couldn't hurt, right?

It took about 6 months to a year of taking herbal supplements and following the diet before I started noticing a change. My dizziness started to decrease and my black outs reduced in number. I then noticed that I was able to walk to the bathroom on my own. Granted the herbal medicine did not fully heal me 100 percent but they did improve the quality of life that I had. I felt like I could live again. The Lord showed me how to heal physically as well as emotionally! I am just so thankful and praising God that He got me to a point where I could live again! Once again, He was there for me!

I realized during this point in my life that I was putting more faith and trust in people and doctors when I should have been putting faith and trust in God. He is the TRUE healer. I don't know why I was doing that, especially when I had never trusted people before. I should've remembered all of the times I trusted people that ended badly and refused to do it again but instead, I listened to people. I am thankful though that once again God intervened. I could have been sick for far longer than three to four years if He had not spoken to me. Maybe during one of the falls, I could have been seriously injured or the concussions could have been more life threatening. All I can say is Thank you Lord for saving my life once again!

PART 3

THOUGHTS AND FOCUS

CHAPTER 9

Thoughts

Thoughts are very powerful. They affect how we act and they affect our moods. Some might think that they are no big deal but in fact, they are a very strong motivator or discourager. A thought is defined as the action or process of thinking or a serious consideration of a topic or idea ("thought." *Merriam Webster's Collegiate Dictionary, Tenth Edition.* 1995). It is reasoning power or the power to imagine. Whatever your heart desires, that is what you think about. If you think about negative or evil things, than your actions will bring to life what you are thinking about. If you want to be happy and have wonderful things happen in your life, than you need to think on those things.

The Bible says in Provers 23:7 that "For as he thinketh in his heart, so is he:" (*The Holy Bible, Authorized King James Version with Words of Christ in Red*, Holman Bible Publishers, 1998.) As you can see from this passage, your thoughts have great power over who you are. If you want to change yourself and your life, you need to first change your thoughts! Just picture in your mind what you desire for yourself. If you continuously think about it, it will come to pass! If you want love, think on love and it will come to pass! If you want to be healthy, think healthy thoughts and you will be healthy! It first begins with your thoughts!

Help Me Lord
(2008)

How do you quiet the tears?
How do you stop the rain?
What will bring out the sun?
What will ease the pain?

Why can't I start to smile?
Why is the agony so deep?
When will I laugh and play?
When will I cease to weep?

I feel like every rock has fallen
And every tree unturned
I feel as though my mind is screaming
While my heart continuously is burned.

I feel lost and alone
And unable to bear
I feel weak and powerless
And struggle to even care

I start to feel hopeless
While I push to move forward
I continue all of my expectations
But scream and am not being heard.

My heart wants to quit and sink
But my spirit says no
Family aggravates the situation
And only confuses me even more so.

I don't know how to think or feel
I don't know what to say
I don't know how to be cheery
Or make it through a day.

All I know is to simply ask
Some words of my God – please
I'm crying with my heart and soul
Lord – please – help me!

I wrote that poem at one of my dark points. I was saved at the time but I was still struggling with those dark thoughts and depression. I have written many poems. I must admit that most are dark because I wrote them when I felt so hurt. I didn't know how to express my feelings in any way but through poems. I have written love poems though and I also wrote this next poem that actually got published:

Heaven's Window

There is a window
I often look through
It shows a place
That I can't get to.

The place is warm.
The place is bright.
I often find myself
Wanting to run in the light.

The place I see
Is Heaven above.
I ache to be there
To experience the love.

I know Jesus is there.
I can feel Him inside.
Up there I can't run.
Up there I can't hide.

Zoe A Gable
Copyright 2002

Yes I struggled with dark thoughts back then but I also knew that He was still there. He always had a pull on my heart and every time I started to feel down, He always knew how to cheer me up.

I especially remember one instance when I was working at a lawyer's office. A co-worker and I were not getting along. She was constantly belittling me and making me feel bad. I came home from work that day in tears and ready to quit. As I pulled in the driveway, there must have been one hundred butterflies in a giant ball in my parking spot. As I slowly drew closer, the butterflies encircled my car! I instantly knew that the Lord sent those butterflies to make me smile! It worked because afterwards, I no longer thought about that horrible day. I constantly thought about the wonderful gift the Lord gave me after work to cheer me up!

So you see, if I had kept my thoughts on the events of the day and how horrible that person treated me, I would have been depressed and miserable for the whole day if not many days afterward. Because the Lord sent those butterflies at the perfect moment, I was able to think about their beauty and how loving He is. For the rest of the day, I was happy and smiling.

Yes we all have horrible days but it's our choice to decide whether or not we will let that experience ruin our entire day or let it go and make the best of the rest of the day. If we hold on to that horrible experience, than it is our own fault for being miserable. Yes there may have been a person who did something mean but we shouldn't choose to let that person win by taking our joy away from us all day long! They may have won the moment but they don't have to win the day or ruin our whole life! We can fight back by simply finding a thought, moment, or even person who brightens our day and think on that thing or person instead. We can win our happiness back!

The Bible tells us in Psalm 94:11 that "The LORD knoweth the thoughts of man, that they are vanity." He knows when we are thinking on the wrong things. He knows if we desire lust, money, power, etc. He also knows if we are thinking on pain and sorrow. He feels that pain with us. He wants us to feel love and joy. He gave us free will though. He can't change our thoughts. We have to choose to change them. We have to want to change them. In order to do that, we need to learn what those thoughts are doing to us. Sometimes we are doing something and don't even realize what it's doing to us until it's too late. We feel sad and depressed and don't even realize why! We need to always stop and analyze our thoughts. We need to examine them and determine if they are helpful or hurtful to us. If we choose to keep thinking on the hurtful things, then it's our own fault if we remain sad or depressed!

If we can recognize that those things are hurting us, than we can say "stop" and start thinking about positive things. We may find that the depression and sadness subside because we are no longer thinking about the things that depress us! At first it may be difficult. You need to step out of your comfort zone a little bit and take a minute to analyze the thought. It may take some practice in the beginning but as time goes by, you will find it easier and easier to achieve. I know it sounds simple but sometimes the best things in life are free!

I used to mediate on a Bible verse that would help me determine if I was thinking on the wrong things. It also is from Psalms. It is Psalm 139:23-24 which states "Search me, O God, and know my heart: try me, and know my thoughts: And see if there be any wicked way in me, and lead me in the way everlasting." Some times when we don't know we are thinking the wrong thing, this passage when used as a prayer will help you. You may not realize what your thinking is wrong but He will show you. He can reveal so much to your heart.

Jesus even spoke about thoughts. In Matthew 15:15-20, Jesus explained thoughts this way: "Then answered Peter and said unto him, Declare unto us this parable, and Jesus said, Are ye also yet without understanding? Do not ye yet understand, that whatsoever entereth in at the mouth goeth into the belly, and is cast out into the draught? But those things which proceed out of the mouth come forth from the heart; and they defile the man. For out of the heart proceed evil thoughts, murders, adulteries, fornications, thefts, false witness, blasphemies: These are the things which defile a man: but to eat with unwashed hands defileth not a man." Your thoughts if they are evil will come out in words and hurt others as well as yourself!

We need to pay attention to what we think about. If we have a thought, we need to discern if it will help or hurt us. Is it a good thought or a bad thought? Did that thought come from the Lord or did it come from our enemy? Before we let that thought fester with us throughout the day, we need to examine it and make sure that it will not destroy us.

In 2 Corinthians 10:1-8, it states: "Now I Paul myself beseech you by the meekness and gentleness of Christ, who in presence am base among you, but being absent am bold toward you: But I beseech you, that I may not be bold when I am present with that confidence, wherewith I think to be bold against some, which think of us as if we walked according to the flesh. For though we walk in the flesh, we do not war after the flesh: (For the weapons of our warfare are not carnal, but mighty through God to the pulling down of strong holds;) Casting down imaginations, and every high thing that exalteth itself against the knowledge of God, and bringing into captivity every thought to the obedience of Christ; And having in a readiness to revenge all disobedience, when your obedience is fulfilled, Do ye look on things after the outward appearance? If any man trust to himself that he is Christ's, let him of himself think this again, that, as he is Christ's, even so are we Christ's. For though I should boast somewhat more of our authority, which the Lord hath given us for edification, and not for your destruction, I should not be ashamed." If we are children of God, than we need to trust His word and examine ourselves and our thoughts and make sure they are pleasing in His eyes.

We should think on happy times and happy things. We should think on love and trust and forgiveness. As it states in Philippians 4:8, "Finally, brethren, whatsoever things are true, whatsoever things are honest, whatsoever things are just, whatsoever things are pure, whatsoever things are lovely, whatsoever things are of good report; if there be any virtue, and if there be any praise, think on these things." The happy thoughts will help us to be happy. The joyful thoughts will fill us with joy. The peaceful times will fill us with peace. The lovely memories will fill us with love. Those things are so much better than the bad times. I would rather have happiness and love than sadness and depression. Wouldn't you?

If you still struggle with your thoughts and wonder if the thoughts are good or bad, than seek His counsel. Kneel before Him and pray. He will help you. As Hebrews reminds us in 4:12, "For the word of God is quick, and powerful, and sharper than any two-edged sword, piercing even to the dividing asunder of soul and spirit, and of the joints and marrow, and is a discerner of the thoughts and intents of the heart."

If you are unable to discern your thoughts as to whether they are good or bad, praying will open up your heart to Him and He will reveal it to you. He will give you that "nudge" that many call your conscious that makes you feel guilty or shameful for the thought. You will know at that moment if the thought is a good one or not.

Another way that may help you discern the thought is by asking if it helps you only or helps others. Many thoughts that come from our heart are vain and selfish. We are human after all. We can't help it. As an example, imagine that you are standing in front of a shoe store and you suddenly have a thought that encourages you to waste bill money to buy these beautiful new pair of shoes. When you think about the benefits, it's clear that the benefit is to you because you want those shoes and you care more about the shoes than paying the bills. You are not thinking of your family who might go without supper so you can have those shoes.

At that moment, you have to choose between your desire for the shoes or your family. As you can see, you can tell from the selfish nature of the thought that it is not a positive thought. You should therefore change your attention away from that thought onto something that will benefit your family and remove yourself from the front of the store and away from the temptation.

I realize that this was a poor example with regard to explaining it but I hope it helped you in some way better understand how to handle examining your thoughts. Please don't be discouraged. We will all come across thoughts that are hard to decipher whether they are good or bad. If you pray and ask yourself that question about benefits, it will become easier and easier to determine in the future. Always remember, you are never alone!

CHAPTER 10

Focus

What can I say about focus? You might think that thoughts and focus are the same thing, but in actuality they are not. Webster's Dictionary defines focus as a center of activity, attraction, or attention or to cause to be concentrated ("focus." *Merriam Webster's Collegiate Dictionary, Tenth Edition.* 1995). To simplify, it would be like having a simple thought of a car but then putting all of your attention on that car – concentrating on every detail of its make and look, noting its color, how big of an engine it has, etc.

Sometimes it is not enough just to examine your thoughts but you also need to examine your focus. We don't often realize it but our negative thoughts also become our focus. We have that "bad day" and not only do we think about it all day, we also play the entire scenario in our minds all day long focusing on every word, our reaction, what we could have done differently, etc.

Yes we should examine our thoughts and weigh them against good and evil but we should also examine our focus. We need to determine if we are thinking on bad things as well as focusing on them continuously throughout the day. A bad thought could just be one thought like buying the shoes at the store in my previous example. I stood in front of the store and thought: "how great would I look in those!" The focus aspect of it would be if I tried to walk away from the store and then afterwards all day I was arguing with myself saying that I have to have those shoes. I need to go back to the store and get them. It begins to disrupt my sleep. It even haunts my dreams. It becomes the only thing important on my mind. I tune out my husband. I tune out my job or my friends. Those shoes are the only thing that I seem to care about.

I say these things about thoughts and focus because the Lord pointed out to me that I was doing these things to myself. All of the years that I spent suffering with depression, etc., were actually me hurting myself! I would have a random bad thought after someone hurt me and instead of erasing it from my mind, I began to dwell on it. It became my whole focus. I started expanding on it and creating horrible worse-case scenarios in my head. When I thought about the past, I was constantly playing the event in my head and trying to create different ways to better handle the situation. What was the point? The event happened years ago. What were the odds that the exact same event would happen again, let alone continuously repeat itself?

The bad part was that I will never have the opportunity to redo those events. I will never go through those moments again so that I can change them! Why did I keep thinking about them? Why did I keep tormenting myself with the pain that I went through? Why did I relive the moment over and over for years? It was almost like I wanted to feel pain.

If I could have just changed my thoughts and focus, I would have found joy and happiness much sooner in life. Instead, I chose to keep thinking about them and focusing on what happened. I kept myself reliving the past and in doing so, I continuously felt the pain it caused. I never allowed myself to forgive and forget. I never allowed myself to talk about them and heal. It was like I wanted to suffer. Deep down I really didn't want to suffer but by choosing to hang on to them, it seemed like I did.

I wanted to feel love and joy so badly. I craved it so deeply but because I refused to stop thinking about my pain, I never allowed it to come into my life. I was sabotaging my own happiness. I was keeping myself from the things I so desperately wanted! It is actually painful to think about that because I kept blaming others for my unhappiness but in actuality, I was the cause of it. I didn't realize that I was tormenting myself until God opened my eyes to that revelation. I always thought they were keeping me miserable and they ruined my life but actually, I was allowing them to do it because I wouldn't let it go.

It's sad to think how much happiness I could have missed out on just because I was unwilling to stop thinking about the past. I hung onto those bad things for years. I have to be careful not to think and focus on that topic now! It will be yet another regret or negative thing that will keep me from happiness.

Sometimes I am amazed to see how easy it is to go down that negative path. I guess that's why it says in Matthew 7:13-14: "Enter ye in at the strait gate: for wide is the gate, and broad is the way, that leadeth to destruction, and many there be which go in there at: Because strait is the gate, and narrow is the way, which leadeth unto life, and few there be that find it."

There are so many things that can distract us from following the correct course. There are events and people that can easily lead us astray. Staying on the straight and narrow path is difficult with so many distractions. We have to stand strong and firm. We need to constantly evaluate ourselves to make sure that we haven't been led astray from the correct path. Any false or wrong deviation from the path will hurt us. It's too easy to get led astray. Oftentimes we are led astray and we don't even realize it has happened until it's too late.

My only words of encouragement to you are to not give up. There is hope – even when you think there is none. I was where you might be. I was ready to die. I even tried to kill myself! Know though that God can make all of the pain go away. Living for Him will be a much greater reward than all of the pain you have felt for so long. His blessings will pour out onto you tenfold! You will be amazed at how He touches your heart. You will be excited to see all of the wonderful things that He has in store for you. You will be shocked to see how great your life will turn out in the end. His plans are greater for you than even you can imagine for yourself. It is something you would have never imagined in your entire lifetime. He is more precious and wonderful than anything or anyone could ever be. If you never trust anyone again, trust Him. I will never be sorry I did.

CHAPTER 11

The Power of His Word

It's amazing to learn about God sometimes. When I read His word and He reveals something to me, I sit amazed because when I read that same passage many times before, the message never had occurred to me. It's definitely true when they say His word is alive. He reveals certain truths to your heart at times when He wants you to know them. He reveals them when He feels you are far enough along in your faith to handle them or when He knows they will help you at that particular point in time.

I began a folder one time with things He has revealed to me. I love to go back to that folder and just remind myself of what He spoke to my heart. Sometimes I find the same Bible passage in the book multiple times and in each revelation, there's something new than the time before. I know God was speaking to my heart during that time. I must have been struggling with something at that moment and what He revealed, helped me during that point in time. I find myself wishing I wrote down my struggles as well. It may help in the future if I find myself in the same predicament.

The power in His word is life changing. It affects my attitudes, my joy, my relationships, and yes even my physical health. Just as a negative thought or focus can keep you in emotional pain, it can also keep you sick and in physical pain.

Many years ago when I prayed to God to be sick, I felt like He answered my prayers. In actuality though, thinking those thoughts made me sick. I wished it upon myself. If my faith was strong and I directed my attention to all of the times Jesus healed in the Bible, I may have avoided the physical pain. I may have avoided the wheelchair. Even if the disease was present, maybe I could have gotten out of the wheelchair sooner!

It's hard to know exactly what might have happened back then. Only God knows for sure and I know that it's not right to "focus" on "what-if's." Instead I try to focus on my health now. Yes I still struggle with health problems. I have faith though that I am healthy and healed in the name of Jesus. He will call me home when He wants me home. He has more work for me to do so until that point in time, I will stay focused on the fact that I am healthy and He is healing me. I want to accomplish all that He has planned for me. I don't want to spend the next half of my life miserable and depressed. I don't want to spend my time worried about what new health problem may happen. I would much rather be happy and stay focused on Him. I have wasted too much of my life already.

Keeping the positive thoughts in your mind will also keep your attitude positive. When fear creeps in, I start to worry. If I remain positive, bad things can happen but I handle them with my head held high. I know that I don't need to worry. God will get me through it. He is with me holding my hand. All I need to do is lean on Him and everything will be okay.

I remember back when my husband and I lived in that apartment. We struggled greatly back then financially. We both had trouble finding and keeping work. The work we did have didn't pay a whole lot so 99 percent of our income went to rent. We never had money for groceries. There was one month where we lived on a bag of potatoes. To this day, we struggle with eating a baked potato. We lived on them and nothing else for a whole month and the thought of eating another one was horrifying. One thing I am thankful during that time period is that my husband and I never worried or panicked over money. We always knew that God would provide somehow. Yes we may have eaten the potatoes with a frown on our face but we were always thankful that we had something to eat at all. I cannot count how many times we would open our front door to find multiple bags of groceries on our door step. I always cried tears of joy knowing that once again He was providing for us. As long as we kept the faith, we never went hungry and we always had a roof over our heads.

In 2001 we purchased a mobile home on five acres. It was out in the country and I loved to watch the different wildlife in our yard. I woke up at 6 am each morning to find deer and turkey in the yard and I was amazed to just watch them. It was so peaceful and relaxing. It was at this property that I dealt with the health problems and the wheelchair. I was forced to leave my job and we began to struggle making the mortgage payments. Even though I was depressed and thought of dying many times, I never worried about bills. We started to receive support and financial help from family. His family helped us catch up on the utilities while my family helped us with groceries and the mortgage. I still believed even during this point that He would provide.

Finally after three years, the Lord blessed me with disability. What shocked me was how quickly the response happened. I had heard from so many people that it may take months if not years to get an answer and even then, I may have to appeal it. The Lord was watching out for us though and we received a positive outcome within weeks of the hearing. I cried tears of joy once again and our financial concerns were no longer a problem. We actually started to get ahead a little bit and I know it was all His doing.

I share these examples to show you just how much He cares and watches over us. We may not think He's watching, but He's always there. He knows what your concerns are even before you do. All you need to do is trust Him. He always has great plans in store for you.

We will always find hardship on this earth whether it be financial, physical, loss of a loved one, or emotional but the hardship will not last forever. It feels like eternity while we're in the moment but in actuality, it doesn't take that long at all. It's hard to do sometimes but we must stay strong and have faith in Him. He will guide us through it and as long as we listen to His guidance and seek

Him, we will come out of it victorious and stronger than ever. I have found that every hardship is a great blessing and lesson to be learned. It also builds character and teaches me how to deal with the next mountain that comes my way.

CHAPTER 12

The Right Path

For many of us, life takes us on many roads. We start out as little ones learning to talk and walk. We grow to teenagers believing that we know everything. We then become adults dealing with little ones and teenagers and feeling like we've become our parents. We end up as elders with wisdom and love to share to our grandchildren.

Some may go to college. Some may go straight to work. Whatever the case may be, there will always be challenges. There is no way to avoid it. We struggle with finances. We struggle with temptations. We struggle with loss whether it is loss of loved ones or possession loss. We all have different emotions and different experiences. No one life will ever be completely perfect. God designed your experiences for you. He picked the right things for you that He knew would help you and teach you. All you can do is embrace the good with the bad and try to stay on the right path.

Temptations are always hard. Nowadays it seems like the temptations are that much stronger. The world comes up with more and more things to entice us with and more ways to encourage us to spend money. Sin also seems to gain a larger and larger hold on us. As I quoted earlier with regard to the straight and narrow path, those temptations want to lead us down the wide path – the wrong path. We must stay strong and resist those temptations. We need to follow the narrow path – the right path.

When I decided I wanted to be a writer, I dreamt of writing romance novels. I craved love so badly that I wanted to fantasize about what I thought it was like. I never experienced the real thing so I had to create in my mind what I thought it looked like. I thought the romance novels would give me an outlet for my desire for love and even if I didn't receive it in real life, I could experience it in the fictional one.

As I drew closer to God, He began to give me a desire to write about my past and share my story. It took years for me to build up the courage to complete the task. It wasn't that I didn't want to be obedient to Him. On the contrary, it was the exact opposite. In fact, I started writing this book many years ago when He first prompted me to. My struggle was getting it published for everyone else to see. I didn't realize that He wanted more of me than just writing down my feelings. He wanted me to share my pain.

I have to admit that this terrified me. As I stated much earlier, I was afraid of the ridicule from other people. I was afraid of what others might say about me. As I grew in my faith, I began to realize that obedience is more important to Him than fear. Obedience is a sign of great love to Him. He has shown so much love for me.

Why couldn't I do the same for Him? I had to overcome my fears and show Him just how much I loved Him.

I don't know where you are at in your faith. Maybe you are farther along than I or maybe you don't even know Him that well. Wherever you are, I just want to encourage you to take my words to heart. He meant my story to touch lives as He always does with His word and if I can help someone with my heartache, then to me the pain I endured was worth it. I only want to help and encourage you. I only want to be there for you as He was there for me.

For those of you that may be farther in your faith, I can only say that I hope I will continue to strive to accomplish what you have achieved. I pray that He will continue to guide and teach me as He has done for you. I also pray that you will not let fear stand in the way of sharing your wisdom. You have so many lessons to teach the younger generation. They need your wisdom and guidance to avoid those hard temptations. They need your strength and faith to help them through the struggles. You can share with them what got you through similar situations. Please don't let the enemy keep you from being a blessing to someone. The rest of us need you!

If you don't know Him, then I simply ask why? If you desire a father, go to Him as you would go to your father. If you desire a friend, go to Him as you would a friend. You don't need a special prayer. You don't need to have a pastor present unless you would feel more comfortable with one. All you need is you and Him. You can be anywhere to talk to Him. I have even talked to Him on the toilet before! He doesn't care where you are. He doesn't care about what you're wearing. You don't have to be perfect to go to Him. He loves you just the way you are. All He cares about is your heart. He is wherever you are and He sees you all the time so He knows everything already. You don't have reason to fear.

All you need to do is say something like this to Him out loud:

"Jesus, please forgive me. I know I have sinned against you and I am sorry. I realize that I need you. I want a better life. I want to be loved and be happy. Please come into my heart and life. Please teach me how to live for you. Please help me to be strong. I can't do this on my own anymore, Lord. I need you. In Jesus' name, I pray. Amen."

You don't even have to say those exact words. Say what's in your heart. The only important thing is that you reach out to Him. The words don't matter. He just wants you to come to Him with anything. He wants to bless you. He wants you to let Him love you. Please don't be afraid to be loved.

If you have said the above prayer, I ask that you please reach out to someone. Please contact a loved one or a local pastor and tell them that you said the prayer. If you feel more comfortable, you may also reach out to me. I would be honored to pray with you and assist you on your walk with Christ. Knowing that I touched someone and helped someone makes all this worthwhile. My heart and desire is to serve the Lord and help you. I want to be your friend and sister in Christ. I want to love you as Christ loves you and pray for you. If I can share in your most joyous moment of your life when you gave your heart to the Lord, for me it would be the greatest honor.

I pray that I touched your heart. I pray that my words helped you in some way. I also pray that you choose Him. I encourage you to choose the right path and stay focused on the light. His light will make all of your paths straight.

Printed in the United States
by Baker & Taylor Publisher Services